21st Century
Junior Library

# INFOGRAPHICS:
# TRADE

Christina Hill

## Econo-Graphics Jr.

Published in the United States of America by

## CHERRY LAKE PUBLISHING GROUP
Ann Arbor, Michigan
www.cherrylakepublishing.com

Reading Adviser: Beth Walker Gambro, MS, Ed., Reading Consultant, Yorkville, IL

Photo Credits: Cover, Page 1: ©UnitoneVector; Page 5: ©salarko/Shutterstock; Page 7: ©Paradda Muangnak/Pixabay, ©Lidok_L/Shutterstock; ©SThom/Shutterstock; Page 8: ©jjltd/Getty Images, ©Alejandra Jimenez/Pixabay,: ©Clker-Free-Vector-Images/Pixabay, ©Clker-Free-Vector-Images/Pixabay, ©Maya A. P/Pixabay, ©Mohamed Hassan/Pixabay, ©Robert Król/Pixabay, ©tswedensky/Pixabay, ©GOLDMAN99/Shutterst; ©QuietLuna/Shutterstock; Page 9: ©Evgeniya_Mokeeva/Getty Images, ©judyjump/Shutterstock, ©petrroudny43/Shutterstock, ©CNG Coins, Wikimedia; Page 15: ©Kenji Inoue 2102/Getty Images, ©Anna Zasorina/Shutterstock, ©BigMouse/ Shutterstock, ©Nadzin/Shutterstock; Page 16: ©Sasha Wallis/Shutterstock, ©spline_x/Shutterstock, ©Victoria Sergeeva/Shutterstock, ©Shutterstock; Page 18: ©Elena Pimukova/ Shutterstock, ©Iconic Bestiary/Shutterstock, ©SurfsUp/Shutterstock, ©Shutterstock; Page 19: ©Irina_Strelnikova/Getty Images, ©Lyudinka/ Getty Images, ©Dn Br/Shutterstock, ©Ivan Dubovik/Shutterstock, ©MoonSplinters/Shutterstock; Page 21: ©mathisworks/Getty Images, ©Designbek/Shutterstock; Page 22: ©bennyb/Getty Images

**Cherry Lake Press** is an imprint of Cherry Lake Publishing Group.

**Library of Congress Cataloging-in-Publication Data**
Names: Hill, Christina, author.
Title: Infographics. Trade / Christina Hill.
Other titles: Trade
Description: Ann Arbor, Michigan : Cherry Lake Publishing, [2023] | Series: Econo-graphics Jr. | Includes bibliographical references and index.
   | Audience: Grades 2-3 | Summary: "How does trade work? In the Econo-Graphics Jr. series, young readers will examine economy-related
   issues from many angles, all portrayed through visual elements. Income, budgeting, investing, supply and demand, global markets, inflation,
   and more are covered. Each book highlights pandemic-era impacts as well. Created with developing readers in mind, charts, graphs, maps,
   infographics provide key content in an engaging and accessible way. Books include an activity, glossary, index, suggested reading and websi
   and a bibliography"— Provided by publisher.
Identifiers: LCCN 2022037924 | ISBN 9781668919248 (hardcover) | ISBN 9781668920268 (paperback) | ISBN 9781668921593 (ebook) |
   ISBN 9781668922927 (pdf)
Subjects: LCSH: United States—Commerce—Juvenile literature. | Commerce—Juvenile literature.
Classification: LCC HF3021 .H65 2023 | DDC 338.0973—dc23/eng/20220824
LC record available at https://lccn.loc.gov/2022037924
Cherry Lake Publishing Group would like to acknowledge the work of the Partnership for 21st Century Learning, a network of Battelle for Kids.
Please visit http://www.battelleforkids.org/networks/p21 for more information.

Printed in the United States of America
Corporate Graphics

Before embracing a career as an author, **Christina Hill** received a bachelor's degree in English from the University of California, Irvine, and a graduate degree in literature from California State University, Long Beach. When she is not writing about various subjects from sports to economics, Christina can be found hiking, mastering yoga handstands, or curled up with a classic novel. Christina lives in sunny Southern Califo with her husband, two sons, and beloved dog, Pepper Riley.

CHERRY LAKE PRESS

# CONTENTS

# WHAT IS TRADE?

**Trade** is the buying and selling of goods and services. Trade is helpful because it gives people more choices. Markets and stores sell goods from around the world.

Most goods and services are paid for with **currency**. Examples include coins and bills, credit cards, electronic money, and **cryptocurrency**.

# Fast Fact

The car company Tesla said bitcoins could be used to purchase their cars. This happened in 2021. Bitcoin is a form of cryptocurrency. The Model S cost about 2.69 bitcoins. That is equal to $149,990.

2021, CNBC

# Methods of Payment Through Time

| | |
|---|---|
| Pre-money | **bartering** |
| ~600 BCE | metal coins |
| ~600 CE | paper money first used in China |
| 1690 | paper money first used in the American Colonies |
| 1959 | plastic credit cards (American Express) |
| 1998 | e-commerce payment systems (PayPal) |
| 2009 | cryptocurrency (Bitcoin) |
| 2014 | mobile wallets (Apple Pay) |

2022, Cardknox

# THE HISTORY OF TRADE

Long ago, people used what they had as money. People used crops, furs, salt, and even weapons as money. This is called the **medium of exchange**.

People saw there were different goods all over the world. They wanted these different goods. This led to more exploring across the globe. But people could only trade with what others wanted. Coins and paper bills are today's medium of exchange. This has made trade easier.

# Medium of Exchange

Any item can be used as a medium of exchange. It must be desired by another trader. Both sides must agree on its worth.

# What Was a Beaver Pelt Worth?

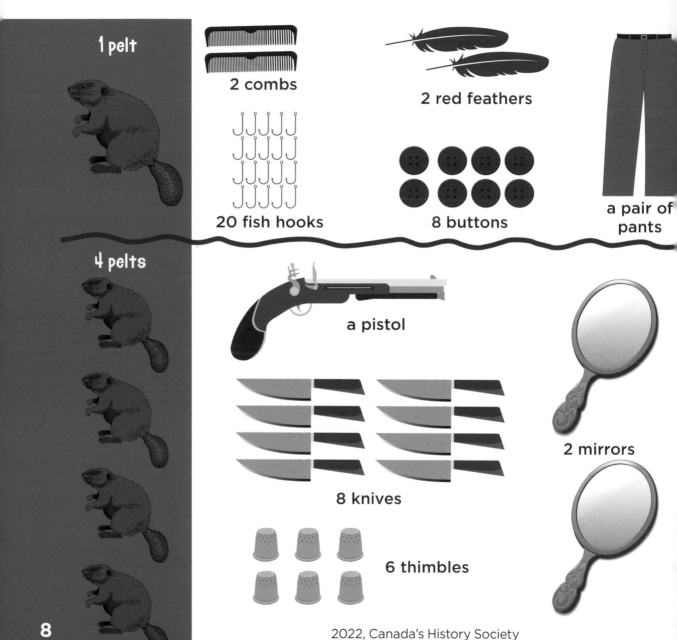

**1 pelt**

2 combs

20 fish hooks

2 red feathers

8 buttons

a pair of pants

**4 pelts**

a pistol

8 knives

6 thimbles

2 mirrors

# The First Coin

The first coin was made as a form of currency. It was made in the seventh century BCE in Lydia. Lydia is now Turkey. The coin was called the stater.

Staters weighed as much as 220 grains of wheat.

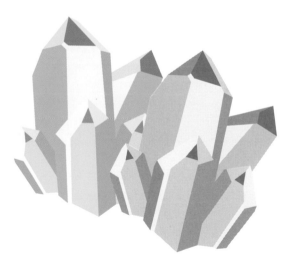

Staters were a mix of 55% gold and 45% silver.

me historians believe 1 stater could have purchased about 30 sheep.

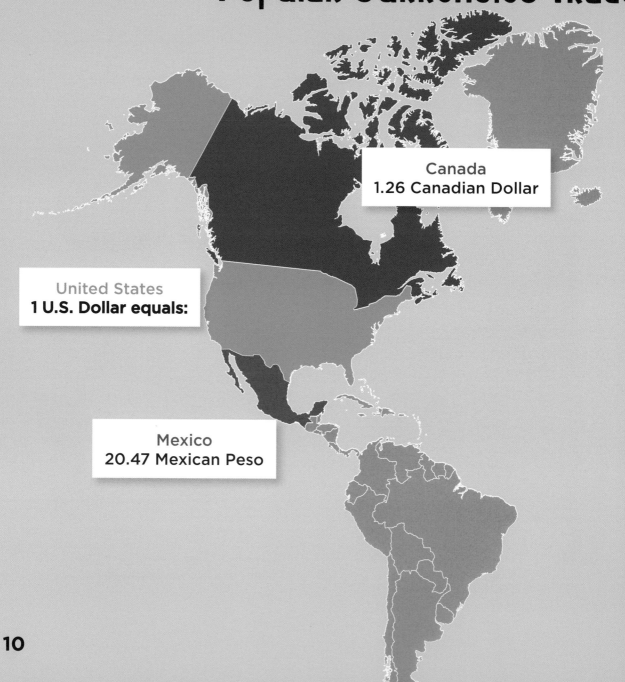

Canada
1.26 Canadian Dollar

United States
1 U.S. Dollar equals:

Mexico
20.47 Mexican Peso

# Around the World

**United Kingdom**
.36 British Pound

**Sweden**
9.19 Swedish Krona

**China**
6.34 Chinese Yuan

**Switzerland**
.91 Swiss Franc

**Europe**
1.13 Euro

**Japan**
113.72 Japanese Yen

**Australia**
.72 Australian Dollar

*Exchange rates as of January 27, 2022*
Federal Reserve

# U.S. EXPORTS

**Exports** are important to a country's economy. Not all countries can make their **consumers** happy. One country might make too much of an item. It can export or sell it to another country. Another country may need or want it.

The United States is big on exports. Its land is full of natural resources. It has factories that make many types of goods. The country also exports services. Workers travel around the world to share their knowledge.

# Which U.S. State Exports the Most?

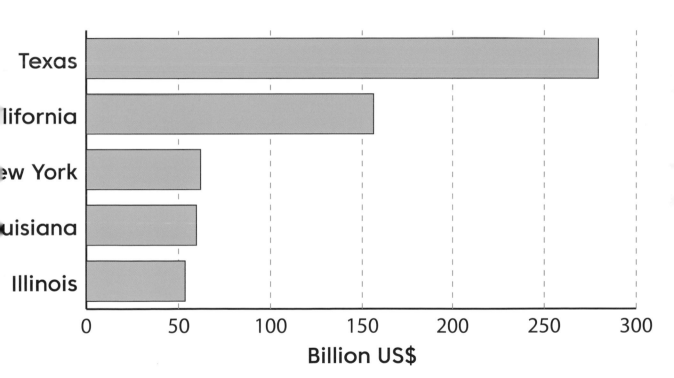

Aircraft

Cigarettes

Computer Processors

Computer Memory

Disodium Carbonate

Gold

Gold

Electronics

Aircraft

Aircraft

Computer Processors

Zinc

Aircraft Parts

Aircraft

Computer
Processors

Lobsters

al
es

Aircraft

Trucks

Gold

Diamond
Jewelry

Silver
Powder

orn

Refined
Oil

Medicine

Aircraft

Coal

Aircraft

Refined Oil

Medicine

Trucks

Coal

Aircraft

Aircraft

Aircraft

Soybeans

Aircraft

Medical
Equipment

Aircraft

Aircraft

| | Vehicles |
| | Aircraft |
| | Mined Goods |
| | Computers and Electronics |
| | Medicine and Medical Supplies |
| | Food |
| | Cigarettes |

Aircraft

Refined
Oil

Cars

Aircraft

Soybeans

Aircraft

2016, U.S. Census Bureau

# Top U.S. Agricultural Exports

The United States exported $146 billion in agriculture in 2020.

## Soybeans
**$25.7 billion**

## Corn
**$9.2 billion**

## Tree Nuts
**$8.4 billion**

## Pork
**$7.7 billion**

# U.S. IMPORTS

The United States **imports** more goods than any other country. Sometimes the **demand** for certain goods is high. But they are hard to produce in the United States. The country then imports them.

The United States imports 15% of its food from other countries. Chocolate, coffee, avocados, bananas, and cars are leading U.S. imports.

# What Imports Are Americans Buying? (2021)

## Machinery and Computers
**$428.8 billion**

## Electrical Equipment
**$416 billion**

## Vehicles
**$283.1 billion**

## Medication and Medical Supplies
**$149.5 billion**

2021, World's Top Exports

## Mineral Fuels
### $223.9 billion

## Gems and Precious Metals
### $96 billion

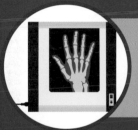

## Medical Devices
### $106.2 billion

## Furniture and Home Goods
### $81.4 billion

## Plastics
### $82.5 billion

# INTERNATIONAL TRADE

Goods and services are bought and sold around the world. This is called international trade. Countries focus on making goods that are easy to make. They import things that are hard for them to make.

# How International Trade Works

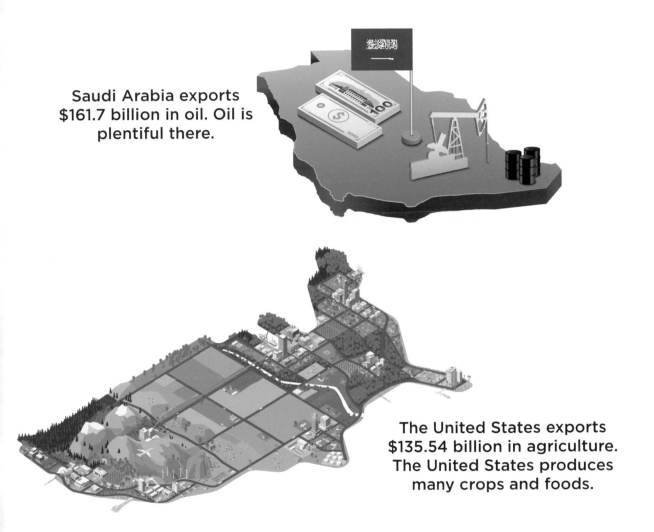

Saudi Arabia exports $161.7 billion in oil. Oil is plentiful there.

The United States exports $135.54 billion in agriculture. The United States produces many crops and foods.

The two countries help each other. The United States exports $1.3 billion of agricultural products to Saudi Arabia. It imports 356,000 barrels of oil per day from Saudi Arabia.

# ACTIVITY
## Where Was It Made?

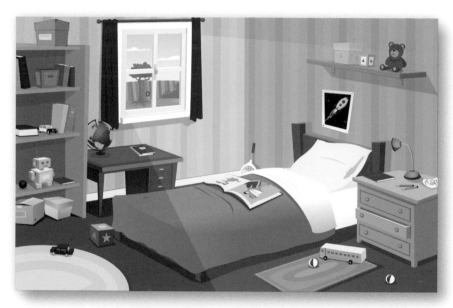

Make a list of at least 15 different items in your room or home. Include your backpack, shoes, clothes, TV, snacks, and any electronics. Find out where each item was made. Look on tags and packaging. Try searching for the company online.

Use the list to create a bar graph. If your items are made in the United States, list the states.

- How many of your items were made in the United States?
- Which country other than the United States made most of your items? Why do you think this is?

# LEARN MORE

## Books

gen, Rachel. *Trade in Our Global Community.* New York: Crabtree Publishing
mpany, 2018.

den, Charlie. *Fair Trade and Global Economy.* New York: Crabtree Publishing
mpany, 2018.

## Websites

**tannica Kids: Trade**
s.britannica.com/kids/article/trade/353871

**dle: International Trade Facts for Kids**
s.kiddle.co/International_trade

## Bibliography

e Editors of Encyclopedia Britannica. "*Free Trade.*" Last modified December 22,
21. https://www.britannica.com/topic/free-trade

Grath, Brian S. "*Trade Battle.*" September 28, 2018. https://www.timeforkids.com/
4/trade-battle/?rl=en-770

pelasis, A. A., Charles E. McLure, Moses L. Pava, and Gabriel Smith. "*Tariff.*" Last
odified March 29, 2022. https://www.britannica.com/topic/tariff

# GLOSSARY

**bartering** (BAHR-tuhr-ing) trading goods or services instead of using money

**consumers** (kuhn-SOO-muhrz) people who buy goods and services

**cryptocurrency** (krip-toh-KUHR-uhn-see) form of currency that exists digitally

**currency** (KUHR-uhn-see) form of money that a country uses

**demand** (dih-MAND) desire to purchase goods and services

**exports** (EK-sports) goods that are sold to another country; to export is to send goods to another country

**imports** (IM-ports) goods bought from another country; to import is to bring in goods from another country

**medium of exchange** (MEE-dee-uhm UHV iks-CHAYNJ) any item that is widely acceptable in exchange for goods and services

**trade** (TRAYD) activity or process of buying, selling, and exchanging goods or services

# INDEX